Cock-A-Doodle-Doo!

What Does It Sound Like To You?

CALVIN~
CHOO CHOO CHUG CHUG
YOU'RE WONDERFUL
I LOVE YOU!
AUNT GeorgeAnne

For Laurie and Zachary.
— M.R.

For Page and Alec.
— S.J.

Text copyright © 1993 Marc Robinson

Illustrations copyright © 1993 Steve Jenkins

Published in 1993
by Stewart, Tabori & Chang, Inc.
575 Broadway, New York, NY 10012

Robinson, Marc. COCK-A-DOODLE DOO! : What does it sound like to you?
text by Marc Robinson; illustrations by Steve Jenkins. p. cm.
Summary: Discusses the words various languages, including English, Spanish, Chinese,
and Hebrew, use for such sounds as a dog's bark, a train's whistle, and water dripping.
ISBN 1-55670-267-1: $12.95
1. Onomatopoeia—Juvenile literature. 2. Animal sounds—Juvenile literature.
[1. Language and languages. 2. Sounds, Words for. 3. Animal sounds.]
I. Jenkins, Steve, ill. II. Title. P119.R63 1993 418--dc20 92-30961 CIP

Distributed in the U.S. by
Workman Publishing
708 Broadway
New York, New York 10003

Distributed in Canada by
Canadian Manda Group
P.O. Box 920
Station U Toronto,
Ontario M8Z 5P9

Printed in Singapore

10 9 8 7 6 5 4 3 2 1

Cock-A-Doodle-Doo!
What Does It Sound Like To You?

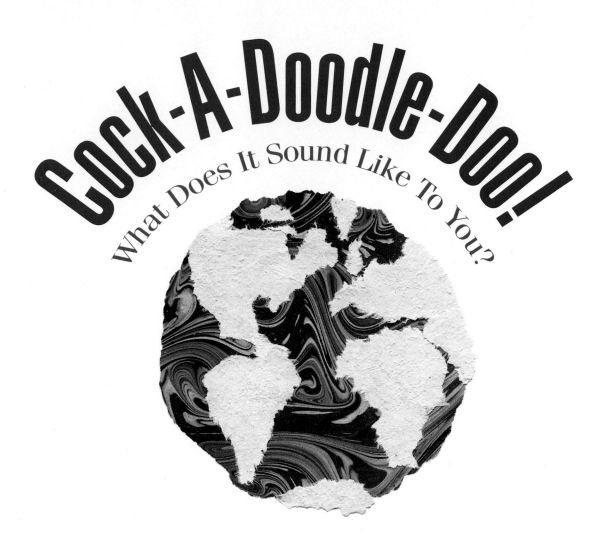

Text by Marc Robinson
Illustrations by Steve Jenkins

Stewart, Tabori & Chang
New York

Does a rooster always crow
COCK-A-DOODLE-DOO?
To me it does — and maybe
to you, too.

COCK-A-DOODLE-DOO!

But to Spaniards roosters cry KEE-KEE-REE-KEE!
Now how, can you tell me, just how can that be?

KEE-KEE-REE-KEE!

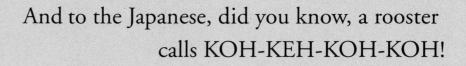

And to the Japanese, did you know, a rooster
calls KOH-KEH-KOH-KOH!

KOH-KEH-KOH-KOH!

To me trains shout CHOO! CHOO! Don't ask me why.

CHOO!

CHOO!

So how could they whistle
TOOT! TOOT!
when they pass
French people by?

And blow STOOK! STOOK! to Russians when they want to say hi?

Why would an English dog
bark BOW WOW!

BOW
WOW!

GUV! GUV!

While a Greek dog
barks GUV GUV?

While an
Indian dog
barks
HOW HOW?

How!

How!

How!

How!
How!
How!

KROO KROO is the sound of a Swahili frog…

In Japanese it's
GEDO GEDO…

GEDO! GEDO!

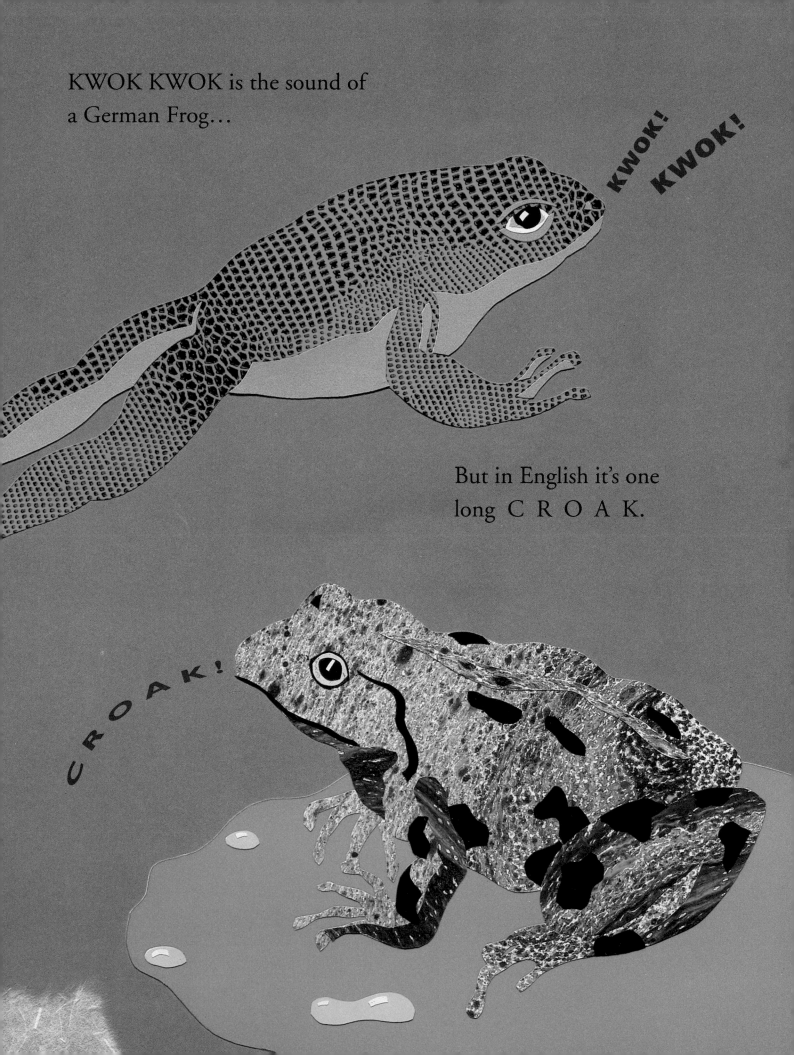

KWOK KWOK is the sound of
a German Frog...

KWOK! KWOK!

But in English it's one
long C R O A K.

CROAK!

BZZZ! BZZZ!
say English bees
whenever they
zoom by, and

BZZZ! BZZZ!

ZMMM! ZMMM! is what
Hebrew bees sing as they fly.

HMMM! HMMM!

If all
bees buzz
the same as the bees
I know from here,
why would bees go
HMMM! HMMM!
past Indian
people's
ears?

Drops of water
I hear go
DRIP
DRIP
DRIP

DRIP

But to
Spanish-speaking
people they go
TIP
TIP
TIP.

TIP

PLEEN
PLEEN
PLEEN
is what
the
Portuguese
hear.

PLEEN!

PLEEN!

PLEEN!

But in
Japan
POTO
POTO
means
falling
water's
near.

POTO!

POTO!

If when I hit my
hammer it pounds
BANG! BANG! BANG!
Shouldn't every other
hammer BANG BANG
the same?

ENGO!

ENGO!

Then why is
ENGO! ENGO!
what some
Africans say?

And a booming
TOOK! TOOK!
is the Russian
hammer's way?

BANG!
BANG!

TOOK!

TOOK!

The answers that we seek
lie in the ways we learn
to speak, and the sounds
that we hear, which are
different ear to ear.

In French, English, Hindi,
in Russian and Portugese,
in Greek, German, Swahili,
and even in Chinese,
from Spain to Japan and
from Israel to here,
sounds sound differently
to each and every
person's ear.

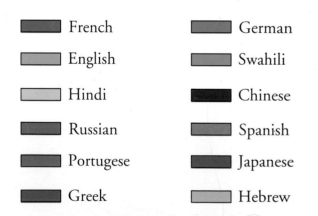

French		German	
English		Swahili	
Hindi		Chinese	
Russian		Spanish	
Portugese		Japanese	
Greek		Hebrew	

Design by Jenkins & Page, New York, NY.
Text composed with QuarkXpress 3.1 and Adobe Illustrator 3.2.
Printed and Bound by Tien Wah Press (Pte.), Ltd., Singapore.